New and Revised Edition

Football Rules IN PICTURES

Edited by Don Schiffer and Lud Duroska

Foreword by **Mel Hein** SUPERVISOR OF OFFICIALS,
AMERICAN FOOTBALL CONFERENCE

Introduction by **Clary Anderson** PRESIDENT,
NEW JERSEY INTER-SCHOLASTIC COACHES ASSOCIATION

Illustrated by George Kraynak

GROSSET & DUNLAP PUBLISHERS NEW YORK

FOOTBALL RULES IN PICTURES

LIBRARY OF CONGRESS CATALOG CARD NUMBER: 72-86663

ISBN: 0-448-01785-7 (TRADE EDITION)
ISBN: 0-448-07611-X (LIBRARY EDITION)
1973 PRINTING

Dedicated to
Helen, Marilyn and Jeffrey

The authors wish to express their appreciation of the help given so generously by the National Collegiate Athletic Association; the National Federation of State High School Athletic Associations; the National Football League, Jim Heffernan, Jack Horrigan and Mel Hein; and Steve Gerdy.

A GREAT SPORT

Football, on the field and off, has been the dominant factor in my life. It has taught me discipline and team play . . . it has taught me that there are winners and losers, and that winners don't always keep winning, nor do losers always keep losing.

I can think of no better training for a productive life than competition in football on the high school, college and professional levels. The sport demands desire and ability to take the initiative. Strength is necessary but so is courage. Characteristics like these are most necessary if a man is to lead a productive and meaningful life for himself and his family.

Persons in the stands profit from football, too, and this goes beyond those few hours of entertainment. They are made aware of the necessity of a man's combining his top physical and mental qualities for ultimate success. Brought home, too, as they watch the flow of action which has been described as everything from a master chess game to a "war without casualties" is the realization that, all things being equal, eleven men attuned to each other and aware of the other man's position must ultimately come out ahead of eleven individualists.

MEL HEIN
Supervisor of Officials
American Football Conference

Mel Hein, All-America at Washington State, starred for fifteen years, 1931–45, as center and linebacker (those were pre-two-platoon days) for the New York Giants. In 1938 he was voted the Most Valuable Player in the National Football League, the only interior lineman to be so honored. He is a member of both the College and Pro Football Halls of Fame, and was a charter member of the Pro Football Hall of Fame.

CONTENTS

THE IMPORTANCE OF KNOWING THE RULES

In the courtroom a Judge often has to tell an offender that "Ignorance of the Law is no excuse." How true in sports!

I doubt that there is a coach who doesn't remember a game that was lost because a player didn't know a rule and committed a violation. The player's intentions may have been thoroughly honest, but the officials have to go by the "law" — the rules of the game — and the needless penalty determined the outcome of the contest.

That is one of the reasons why a book such as this one, devoted as it is to interpreting and clarifying the fundamental rules of football, is an important aid to the player who is learning the game. Through the illustrations and the explanations, he learns what can and what cannot be done. The devise of having offensive players in white jerseys and the defensive players in black helps make the action easier to follow.

The more thoroughly a player learns the rules right from the start, the better equipped he is as a competitor, and the less likely he is to make mistakes. And mistakes cost ballgames.

But this book is not only for the player. It is also for the football fan. By becoming more familiar with the rules and particularly with the official's signals, the spectator in the stands and the spectator at home before his TV screen can better understand what is going on and why. The spectator's enjoyment of the game increases with his knowledge.

Rules were created and are enforced to insure fair play for both teams. Football wouldn't be a sport without them — it's essential that we know the rules and use them properly.

CLARY ANDERSON

Clary Anderson is a former member of the National Rules Committee and currently Athletic Director, football and baseball coach at Montclair High School (New Jersey). He has been a successful football coach for the past quarter of a century, with a winning record of 92%. He is the author of *Make the Team In Football*

RULE DIFFERENCES

The rules illustrated and interpreted in this book are fundamental and apply to high school, college and professional football. In all three areas the basic rules are the same, although the different wording may sometimes lead to confusion. In extracting the essential meaning and purpose of the key rules, the editors relied on a variety of codes, including those used in the National Collegiate Athletic Association, the National Federation of State High School Athletic Associations, the National Football League and the American Football League.

Unlike baseball where the rules are basically the same whether the game is played by high school, college or professional teams, football has never quite achieved such complete uniformity and codification. In large measure this is due to the rugged nature of the sport and the type of play mature professionals may engage in is not always advisable for high school boys. Yet another reason is the constantly changing nature of gridiron strategy through the years, such as the greater use of the forward pass today as compared with the game of the previous generation.

While football has been undergoing continuous changes, baseball is played today just about the way it was played in grandfather's day. But grandfather, and even Dad, would be astounded at how different modern football is from the game he knew.

Take the field itself. Can a fan, entering an unfamiliar stadium, know whether he is about to see a high school, college or professional game? If he is observant, he can. The field, the yard lines and the markers provide no clue—they're the same on each level of competition. But there is a "giveaway"—the different types of goal posts and their location.

If the goal posts are the traditional H-shaped and are set on the end line (10 yards in back of the goal line) of each end zone, then it's either a high school or college game. The fan may be able to tell which it is by noting how far apart the uprights are. In high school football—and the same is true for the pros—the crossbar between the uprights measures 18 feet 6 inches; in college the bar is nearly 5 feet longer, with the uprights 23 feet 4 inches apart. There is one exception. High school teams may use the college-type goal posts if the field is so equipped.

It's much easier to know it's a professional game since the two leagues started using the single curved pole that supports the crossbar and uprights, which are directly above the goal line. Before that, the basic difference was the location of the goal posts.

In 1933 the National Football League relocated the goal posts on the goal line where they have remained ever since in all professional leagues. This change in the rules resulted from a desire to increase interest and action. By shortening the distance to the crossbar by 10 yards, opportunities to score field-goals were improved. The results were as expected. The three-point attempt became such a key scoring weapon among the pros that teams began to carry kicking specialists whose careers were based on this particular ability — to kick a field-goal. Greater scoring brought greater excitement to the game.

But the success of the pros in this area did not tempt colleges to follow their example, even for a trial period. Although they originally had the posts on the goal line, college authorities in 1927 moved them back 10 yards, to the end line of the end zone. The reasoning behind this change in the college rules was that the players were more likely to collide with the posts if they were on the goal line. The player's safety prompted the rule change. The professionals are also concerned about the safety of the players. Before the adoption of the single goal post, set 3 yards back of the goal line as less of an obstruction to the action, they required the goal posts to be wrapped in kapot or rubber padding.

Through the years an important source of difference has been the substitution rule, with the pros proving more consistent in this respect than the collegians. After employing the free-substitution rule from 1943 to 1945 because of wartime conditions, the pros adopted the rule—popularly known as the two-platoon rule—permanently in 1950. It allows the teams to substitute without restriction at any time except when the ball is actually in play.

Many observers credit the increasing popularity of professional football to this rule. It has made possible the use of offensive and defensive platoons, enabling players to concentrate their skills on the phase of the game in which they excel. Teams can also compete at full speed since each platoon can rest on the bench when the other platoon is in action. The art of specialization has been refined to such an extent that special platoons go in for specific action, such as the kick-off or the punt.

Colleges have continued experimenting with this rule. They modify it almost every year, sometimes liberalizing, sometimes restricting the manner in which players may enter and re-enter the game. Free substitution is believed to favor the larger schools, which have the greater number of players. An added consideration is the cost of equipment because "two-platooning" does require more players.

Another difference in the rules is scoring the try-for-point after a touchdown. In an attempt to reduce the number of tie games, colleges adopted a two-point rule. If the ball is carried or passed successfully over the goal line — in the same manner as scoring a touchdown — the try counts for 2 points. If the team elects to place-kick (convert) the try, then it is worth only 1 point.

On this rule the two major professional football leagues differ. The American Football League uses the same rule as the colleges, but the National Football League continues to employ the old rule (as do some high schools) which credits 1 point regardless of whether the try is a kick, run or pass.

The colleges also spot the ball for the try after touchdown on the 3-yard line while high schools and the professionals spot the ball on the 2-yard line.

On running plays, the colleges and high schools differ from the pros as to whether the runner may continue after he slips or falls to the ground without being tackled. The professionals permit the runner to continue — even though his knee, for example, may have touched the ground — so long as contact has not been made by a defensive player. The runner may not advance, under college and high school rules, after any part of his body except his hands and feet touches the ground.

A last basic difference concerns the recovery of fumbles. All three sets of rules permit any player from either team to advance with a fumble if the ball is caught in the air. When the fumble has touched the ground, the college rule states that only the team that has fumbled can advance the ball. The opposing team can only recover it. Under professional and high school rules a fumble may be picked up and advanced by any player on either team.

DEFINITIONS OF TERMS

Batting: Striking the ball intentionally with a hand or arm. It is permissible for any player eligible to touch a forward pass to bat the ball while the pass is in the air. It is also permissible to bat the ball if the player is blocking a punt. In other cases of a free ball, batting is illegal. The penalty is 15 yards.

Blocker: A player using his body to obstruct an opponent. An offensive blocker must observe the restrictions on the use of hands and arms.

Clipping: A type of block in which the player runs or dives into the back or the back of the legs of an opponent other than the runner. Clipping is legal in line play if it done in a rectangular area which is 4 yards wide on each side of the middle offensive lineman and 3 yards deep on either side of the scrimmage line. In the open field clipping is illegal. The penalty is 15 yards from the spot of the foul.

Crawling: An attempt by the runner to advance the ball after he has been tackled. The penalty is 5 yards.

Delay of Game: Any failure by a team to be ready for play within the specified time limit or any action that prolongs the game. The penalty is 5 yards.

Double Foul: When both teams commit fouls and the penalties offset each other.

Down: The unit of play. When a team has first down, it has four plays, or downs, in which to gain 10 yards to retain possession of the ball. If the first down is within the opponent's 10-yard line, then the team has four downs to gain the remaining distance to the goal line.

Fair Catch: A receiver of a kick signals for a fair catch by raising one arm directly above his head. He then is protected against being tackled when he makes the catch but gives up his right to advance the ball.

Field Goal: The ball is place-kicked or drop-kicked from scrimmage over the opposing team's crossbar. The kick scores 3 points.

Forward Pass: A pass thrown on a scrimmage play toward the opponent's goal line. Only the offensive team may throw a forward pass, and it must be thrown in or behind the neutral zone.

Foul: Any infraction of the rules that will draw a penalty.

Free Ball: A live ball in play, except for a forward pass, that is not in possession of a player.

Fumble: When a player loses possession of the ball, except when he passes, kicks or hands the ball off.

Goal Line: The line that has to be reached or crossed by the team in possession of the ball in order to score a touchdown. The goal lines separate the end zones from the 100-yard field of play.

Half: The game is divided into two halves, each half is divided into two periods, or quarters. The half is started with a kick-off. Playing time of a half is 30 minutes in College and Professional football, 24 minutes in High School. Teams may leave the field at the end of the first half. Halftime intermission is 15 minutes in High School and College games, 20 minutes in Professional football.

Huddle: Players get together in a group, usually forming a circle, to decide on the strategy and the signals for the next play. The huddle is not limited to the offensive team. The defensive team may also huddle to determine what strategy to follow.

Hurdling: The runner jumps over or attempts to jump over a player who is on his feet in the open field. At the scrimmage line, hurdling is defined as jumping over a player with both feet or both knees foremost. It is illegal and the penalty is 15 yards.

Interception: The catching of any pass by an opponent who is then allowed to run with the ball.

Kicking: a) Drop-kick: The kicker drops the ball and kicks it just as it touches or rises from the ground.

b) Kick-off: The ball is put into play by a place-kick, drop-kick, or with the use of a tee, at the start of the game, the start of the second half, after a field goal or try-for-point after a touchdown. The kick-off takes place from the 40-yard line of the kicking team.

c) Place kick: The ball is held for the kicker by a teammate.

d) Punt: The ball is kicked before it touches the ground on a scrimmage play or as a free kick after a safety is scored.

e) Return-kick: A kick made by a player immediately after catching a kick; it is now seldom used.

Lateral: This is also known as a backward pass. Any player may pass the ball backward or parallel to his goal line to a teammate at any time.

Line-to-gain: The yard line 10 yards in advance of the most forward point of the ball that the team must reach in four downs or lose possession of the ball.

Man-in-motion: One player of the offensive backfield may be in motion before and as the ball is snapped, but he must be moving away from or parallel to the defensive team's goal line. In high school, if the back starts from the scrimmage line, he must stop for one second before going in motion and must be 5 yards in back of the line when the ball is snapped. The pro rule requires the man in motion to start at least 1 yard in back of the scrimmage line. If he is illegally in motion, the penalty is 5 yards.

Multiple Foul: When two or more fouls are committed by a team, the opposing team has a choice of penalties.

Neutral Zone: An area the length of the football that is between the offensive and defensive scrimmage lines.

Offside: When any part of the player's body is beyond his scrimmage line, or his restraining line before the ball is in play.

Out-of-bounds: The area outside the sidelines and endlines including the lines. The ball or a player touching the sideline or endline is considered out-of-bounds.

Period: The total time of the game is divided into four quarters, or periods. In College and Professional football each period lasts 15 minutes; in High School games it is 12 minutes long. Two periods make a half. Play in the first and third period begins with a kick-off. The second and fourth periods start after an exchange of goals, but play is resumed from the point where it was stopped by the end of the previous period. Before the second and fourth periods there is an intermission of one or two minutes, but players are not permitted to leave the field.

Recovering: Gaining possession of the ball after a fumble.

Runner: Player who is in possession of the ball.

Safety: Two points scored by the team not in possession of the ball. Among the ways a safety is scored are: the runner is tackled in his end zone or goes out-of-bounds from the end zone; the offensive team fumbles the ball out-of-bounds from the end zone; the snap from center goes out of the end zone, and the defensive team is responsible for the ball becoming dead in the offensive team's end zone, with the ball still in possession of the offensive team.

Scrimmage: The action that results when a play starts with the center snapping the ball back and ends when the ball is dead.

Scrimmage Line: The imaginary line established for each team by the point of the ball nearest its goal line. The offensive team must have at least 7 players on or within a foot of the scrimmage line. Defensive players may be positioned anywhere behind their scrimmage line.

Shift: When two or more players of the offensive team change position after lining up and before the ball is snapped. After a shift, all offensive players must remain stationary for a second before the snap.

Snap: When the center passes or hands the ball back to a backfield player. Also known as centering the ball.

Tackle: The maneuver by which a defensive player stops the runner by using his hands, arms or body.

Time-out: When play is stopped at the request of either team for a period of 1½ minutes. The time-out may be of longer duration when necessary, such as when medical attention is given to an injured player. The referee also may call timeouts at his discretion.

Touchback: When the offensive team is responsible for putting the ball in the defensive team's end zone while giving up possession of the ball on such plays as the kick-off or punt. After a touchback, the team with the ball starts the next play with a first down on its 20-yard-line.

Touchdown: Six points are scored when a player in possession of the ball reaches the goal line or is in the end zone of the opposing team by running, catching a pass or recovering a fumble.

Try-for-point: The play that follows a touchdown even if time has run out in a period. The team scoring the touchdown has one play from scrimmage in which to run or pass the ball over the goal line or to place or drop-kick the ball over the crossbar. In High School, College and Professional play, a successful kick scores 1 point. In College, American Football League and most High School games, a successful run or pass scores 2 points. In National Football League and some High School games, a successful run or pass scores 1 point.

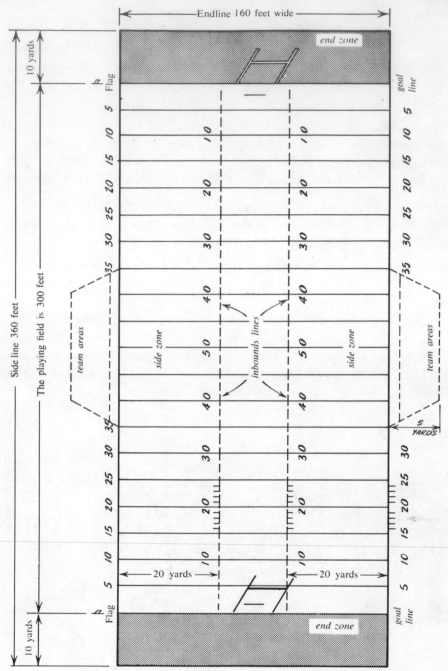

DIAGRAM OF FIELD

THE FIELD

The playing field is 360 feet long and 160 feet wide. When the dimensions are given in yards, the rectangular field is 120 yards long by 53⅓ yards wide. The *goal lines* are 300 feet (100 yards) apart. At each end of the field there is an *end zone,* 30 feet (10 yards) deep. The goal lines, which are located within the end zones, and the end zones are the area in which touchdowns and safeties are scored.

12

The field is marked every 5 yards by a distinct line running across the width of the field from sideline to sideline.

The entire playing field is bordered by a solid line. The area within the sidelines and the endlines is *inbounds*. The sidelines and the endlines themselves, as well as the area beyond these lines, are *out-of-bounds*.

On the field, parallel to the sidelines and, running from goal line to goal line, are two *inbounds lines*. These divide the field into three equal parts, each 53 feet, 4 inches wide. In Professional football the inbounds lines are 60 feet from the sidelines. When a play ends out-of-bounds or in a *side zone* (between the sideline and the inbounds line), the ball is placed at the nearer inbounds line for the next play.

The teams have a place on opposite sides of the field for a players' bench, coaches and other authorized personnel. These are called *team areas* and are located between the 35-yard lines. They are 5 to 6 feet from the sidelines.

Flags with flexible staffs are placed at each corner formed by the goal line and a sideline.

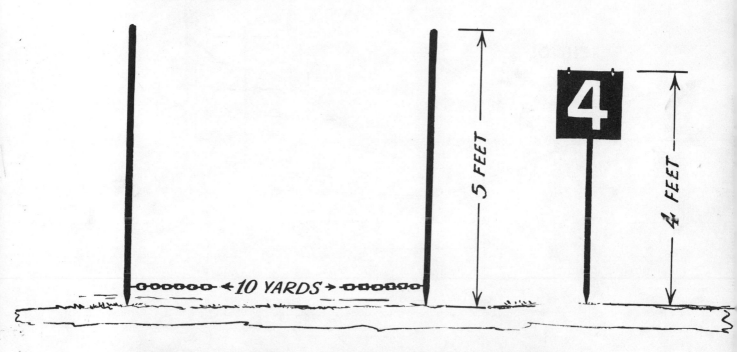

YARDAGE CHAIN AND DOWN MARKER

The *yardage chain* is exactly 10 yards long when fully extended. It is joined to two rods, each at least 5 feet high. It is used to measure if the offensive team has *gained* at·least *10 yards* in *four downs* (plays) or less. When at least 10 yards has been gained, the offensive team has made a *first down* and has four downs again in which to gain another 10 yards.

The *down indicator* is on a rod that is at least 4 feet high and holds four "cards" lettered 1, 2, 3 and 4. The indicator marks the most forward point of the ball at the *start of each down* and the "card" indicating the number of the down is displayed.

13

THE GOAL POSTS

The *goal posts* in High School and College games are located on the end lines; in Professional games, the goal posts are placed on the goal lines. The posts are 18 feet, 6 inches apart in both High School and Professional football. Posts in College games are placed 23 feet, 4 inches apart. In all cases, the *crossbar* is placed 10 feet above the ground. Professional rules require that the goal posts must be *padded* with kapot or foam rubber. "Offset" posts, set behind the goal line but with the crossbar extended to the goal line, are permitted in Professional football.

SCHOOL

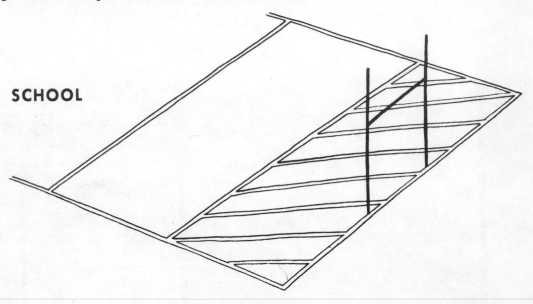

PROFESSIONAL

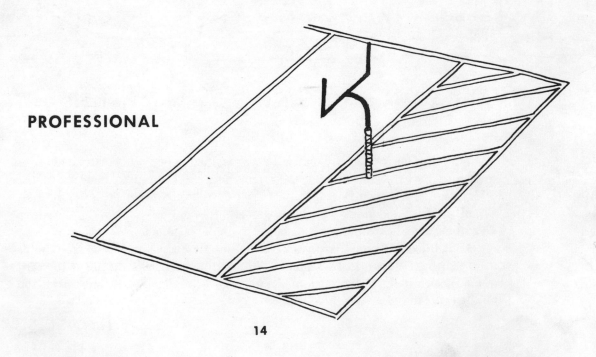

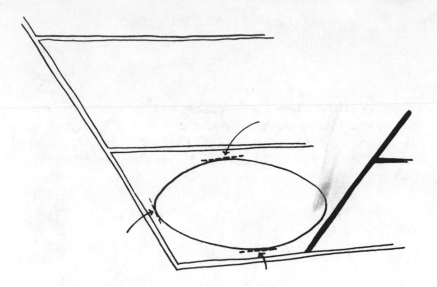

Under College rules, no markings may be placed in the end zones that are closer than 2 feet to the goal line, the endlines or the sidelines.

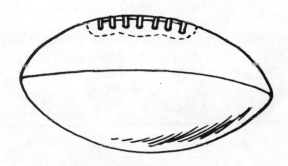

THE FOOTBALL

The football must weigh between 14 and 15 ounces. It is to be inflated to an air pressure of between 12½ and 13½ pounds. The *long circumference* must measure between 28 and 28½ inches. The *short circumference* must be between 21¼ and 21½ inches.

In High School games, the football used, either rubber- or leather-covered, should be of a natural tan color with white 1-inch stripes, 3 to 3½ inches from each end of the football to the near edge of the stripe. Another color may be used with the approval of both teams.

In College games, the football should be of a natural tan color, but a white or colored ball, with or without stripes, may be used for night games.

In Professional games, the football is to be of a natural tan color for day games and of a brown color with white stripes for night games.

STANDARD NUMBERING SYSTEM

To help identify players by position, a *standard numbering system* is *recommended* for High Schools and Colleges. The numbers assigned for *ends* are 80 to 89; for *tackles,* 70 to 79; for *guards,* 60 to 69; for *centers,* 50 to 59; and for *backs,* 10 to 49.

While this numbering system is only *recommended* for High Schools and Colleges, it is *required* in Professional football. There is also a further break-down of numbers for backs in Professional play: *quarterbacks* are to have 1 to 19; *half-backs* 20 to 29 and 40 to 49; and *fullbacks* are to be numbered 30 to 39.

Regardless of his number, however, a player may play any position; in some cases the referee must be notified of the change of position.

IMPROPER EQUIPMENT

A player will be ordered off the field by the official for an improper uniform. In this case, the number on the player's jersey is too small. *Numbers* must be at least *8 inches* high on the front of the jersey, and *10 inches* on the back.

This player will be ordered off the field and not allowed in the game until he has changed his jersey. Any equipment which, in the opinion of the officials, would confuse the opposing players is illegal.

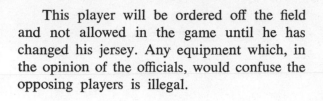

Jerseys or helmets that are similar in color to the football and tend to conceal it are forbidden. The use of camouflage of any sort is illegal and players will not be permitted on the field until the infraction of the rules is corrected.

This player, too, will be ordered off the field because he is too well protected. Players are not permitted to have leather, or other hard material, regardless of how well it is covered or padded, on hands, wrists, forearms or elbows.

Backfield stars have been described as being "slippery as an eel," but any material that helps them achieve such elusiveness is strictly forbidden. The use of oil, grease or any slippery substance on the player's uniform is illegal.

A player will not be allowed in the game if he wears a face mask with sharp edges. Face masks should be of non-breakable, molded plastic with rounded edges or with rubber-covered wire.

OFFICIALS

White circles designate the offensive team; solid black squares show the defensive team. When the play starts at the scrimmage line, the officials take up the positions indicated on the diagram.

BACK JUDGE

UMPIRE

FIELD JUDGE

LINESMAN

REFEREE

THE REFEREE

The *referee* has over-all charge and control of the game. His decisions are final except in those matters specifically under the jurisdiction of other officials. Among his duties are spotting the ball where play is to resume, declaring the ball in play or dead, signalling infractions of rules and pacing off the penalties. He is the authority for the score.

THE UMPIRE

The *umpire* has primary jurisdiction over the equipment and the conduct of the players. In each scrimmage he is particularly responsible for observing illegal play. He must also cover open play that develops after the linemen make their initial charge.

THE LINESMAN

The *linesman* has primary jurisdiction over the neutral zone and infractions (called OFFSIDE) of the scrimmage formation. Under the supervision of the referee, he marks the progress of the ball and keeps an accurate count of the downs. Under his direction assistants operate the yardage chain to mark and hold the starting point and *line-to-gain* for each series of downs as well as the *down indicator*.

THE FIELD JUDGE

The *field judge*, when there is no Back Judge, has primary jurisdiction over the timing of the game. He starts and stops the game clock and keeps the referee informed of the time remaining. He acts for the referee on downfield play.

THE BACK JUDGE

In professional football, the *back judge* takes over the responsibility of timing the game and checks for infractions in his side zone.

The use of a Back Judge is *optional* in College football, but is *required* in Professional.

THE OFFENSE

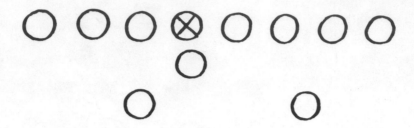

SCRIMMAGE LINE

Count the number of players on the scrimmage line. One man too many? Not at all. An *eight-man line* may be a very rare sight in football, but there is nothing in the rules to make it illegal. This is also true of a nine-man line or a ten-man line. What the rules do require is that there be *at least seven men* on the scrimmage line in order for the formation to be legal. Paul Brown, the former head coach of the Cleveland Browns, once invented and used plays based on an eight-man line.

ILLEGAL FORMATION

This five-man line is illegal under the rules since it does not meet the seven-man minimum required on the scrimmage line.

LEGAL LEG LOCK

It is legal for the two *guards* and the *center* to line up and *lock legs*. The rules permit this, but only for the center and the guards. It is against the rules for other linemen to lock legs. This unusual way for players to line up is not used today for tactical reasons, not because the rules forbid it.

NEUTRAL ZONE

Because one careless player (No. 68), has placed his hand too far forward, the team will draw an *offside* penalty. All linemen except the center are required to be behind their scrimmage line. Only the *center* is allowed to have any part of his body *in the neutral zone*. The neutral zone is measured by the *length of the football* and is the area between the offensive and defensive scrimmage lines. The center, however, is not permitted to be beyond the neutral zone. Should he place himself beyond the neutral zone, the team will draw an offside penalty.

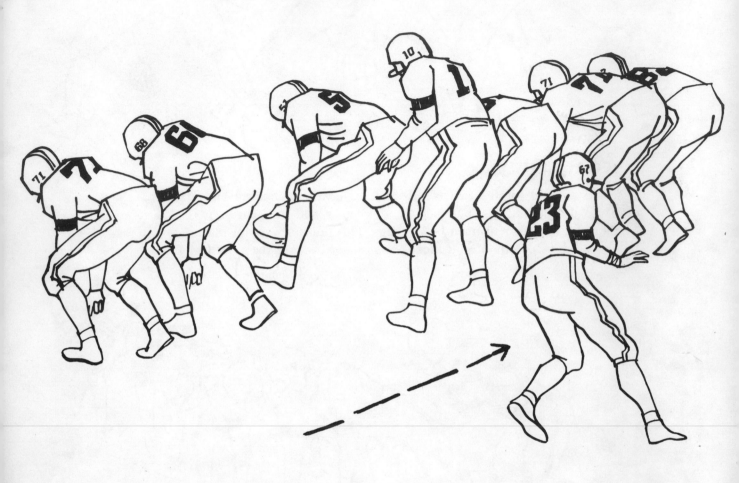

MAN IN MOTION

As this backfield man (No. 23) goes into motion before the ball is snapped, all his teammates must remain stationary because only *one player* is allowed to be in motion. But he became careless as to the direction he is taking. He is moving toward the scrimmage line. In all cases, the man in motion should be traveling a path either parallel to or away from the scrimmage line. Otherwise, his team will be penalized 5 yards.

END IN MOTION

This looks like the start of the old-fashioned end-around play. The end (No. 83) appears to be legally in motion because he is traveling a path backward from the line of scrimmage as the ball is about to be snapped. But the formation is illegal because, having started from the scrimmage line, he has left only six players on the line. The rule requires at least seven linemen. The penalty is 5 yards. It is important to remember that in properly executing one maneuver that infractions of other rules are not committed.

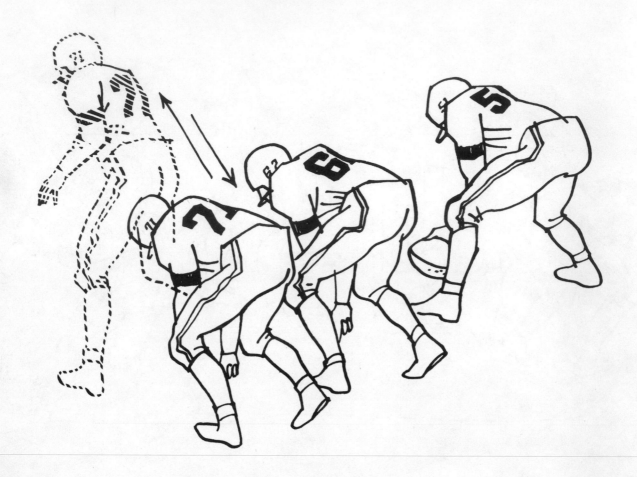

RETURN BEFORE SNAP (Offensive)

An over-anxious lineman (No. 71) has "jumped" the signal and crossed the scrimmage line before the ball is snapped. He immediately recovers and returns to his set position, or three-point stance, without making contact with an opponent. The play still has not started but the lineman is declared to have made a false start. The rule is that once an offensive lineman has assumed a set position, he cannot charge or move in such a way as to lead an opposing player to think the ball is being snapped. The penalty is 5 yards.

RETURN BEFORE SNAP (Defensive)

The defensive lineman (No. 75) has charged into the neutral zone and then has returned to his proper position behind the defensive scrimmage line. Since the ball has not been snapped and no contact was made with an opponent, he is not considered to be offside and there is no penalty. However, if the defensive lineman does this repeatedly after having been warned, he will be penalized 5 yards.

OFFSETTING PENALTIES

If both the offensive and defensive linemen have charged before the ball is snapped, and the official rules that they did so *simultaneously,* then a double foul is called and the penalties offset each other. However, if it is ruled that the action of the offensive player caused his opponent to go offside, then the offensive team will be penalized 5 yards.

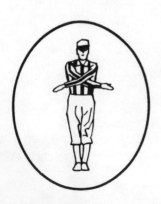

OFFSETTING PENALTIES

The defensive lineman charges into his opponent before the ball is snapped. At the same time the center lifts the football off the ground. While the defensive team will be ruled offside, the center will be penalized for an illegal snap because he is allowed only one *continuous* motion to pass the ball back. Thus the penalties will offset each other.

SNAPPING (CENTERING) THE BALL

Snapping (centering) the ball is the start of every play from scrimmage. If the center doesn't handle this part of the play properly, then the offensive team is in trouble. The center is expected not to raise either end of the ball more than 45 degrees before the snap. He must keep the football pointing toward the opponent's goal line. He must hand or pass the ball back in one continuous motion and is not permitted to fake a snap.

ADVANCING THE BALL

At any time, it is legal for the man with the ball (No. 28) to hand it backward or to pass it backward or to the side (lateral) to a teammate.

28

HANDING BALL FORWARD

The football may be handed forward from one back (No. 17) to another (No. 21) during scrimmage play, but only if *both backs* are *behind the scrimmage line*. If the backs are beyond the scrimmage line, such action is illegal.

HAND-OFF TO LINEMAN

The only occasion on which a lineman is allowed to receive a forward hand-off is illustrated by No. 67. He has turned around so that he faces his own goal line and is at least 1 yard behind the scrimmage line.

THE STIFF-ARM

The ball-carrier (or runner) is employing a standard technique — the stiff arm — to prevent an opponent from tackling him. The ball-carrier is permitted to use his hand or an arm to push away an opponent.

ILLEGAL HELP TO RUNNER

A teammate is trying to help the ball-carrier gain a few more yards. This is illegal and the team will receive a 15-yard penalty. Members of the offensive team are not allowed to push, lift or otherwise assist the runner directly.

A legal shoulder block is being completed upon No. 79. The rule states that a blocker is not permitted to use his hands or arms.

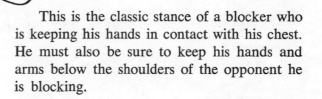

This is the classic stance of a blocker who is keeping his hands in contact with his chest. He must also be sure to keep his hands and arms below the shoulders of the opponent he is blocking.

This blocking technique is illegal. The blocker has forgotten a cardinal rule by locking his hands together. He will be penalized 15 yards for the infraction.

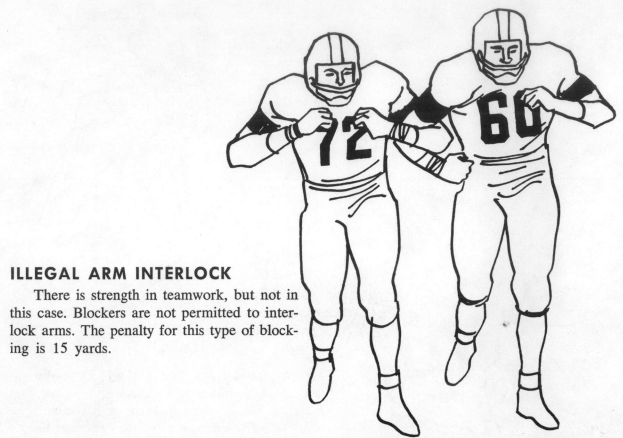

ILLEGAL ARM INTERLOCK

There is strength in teamwork, but not in this case. Blockers are not permitted to interlock arms. The penalty for this type of blocking is 15 yards.

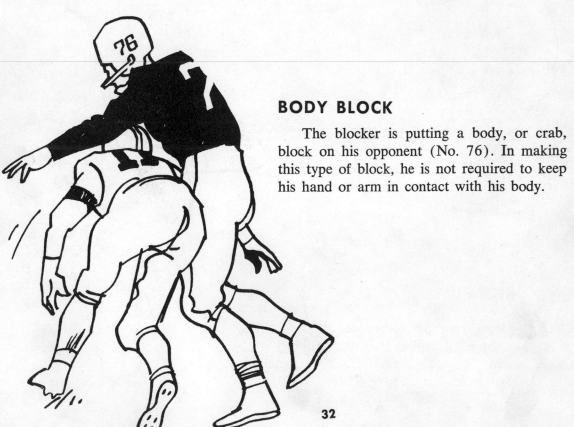

BODY BLOCK

The blocker is putting a body, or crab, block on his opponent (No. 76). In making this type of block, he is not required to keep his hand or arm in contact with his body.

USE OF HANDS

The offensive player (No. 77) is trying to push his opponent (No. 68) with his hands. Such action is in violation of the rule and is punished by a 15-yard penalty. *No blocker is allowed to use his hands to push, pull or grab an opposing player.*

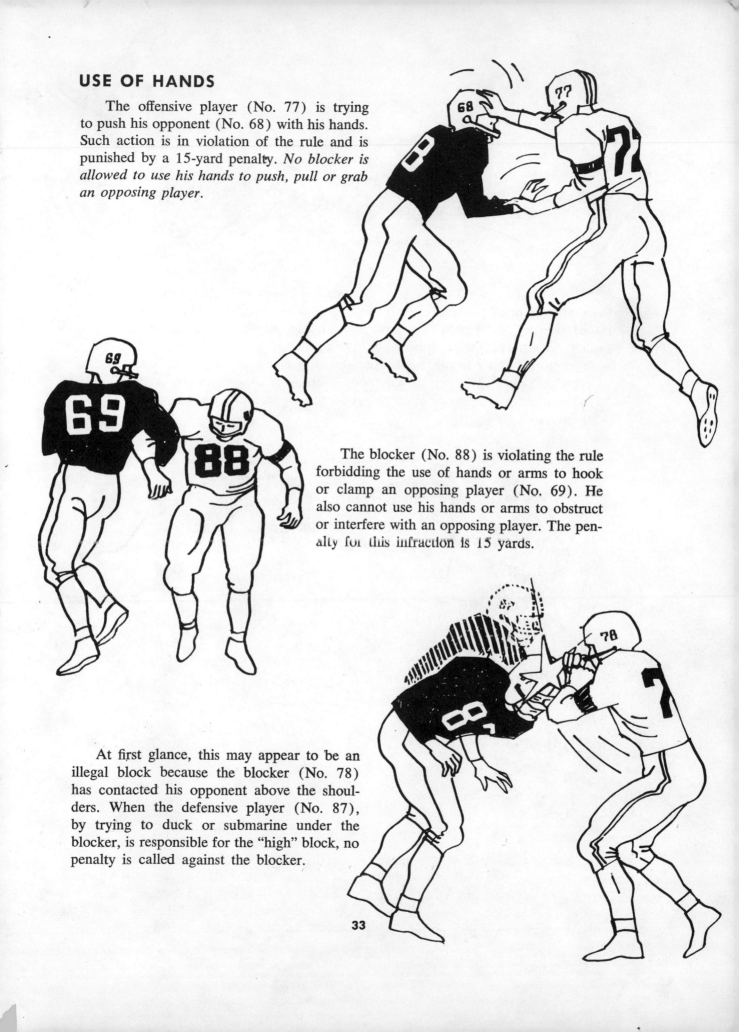

The blocker (No. 88) is violating the rule forbidding the use of hands or arms to hook or clamp an opposing player (No. 69). He also cannot use his hands or arms to obstruct or interfere with an opposing player. The penalty for this infraction is 15 yards.

At first glance, this may appear to be an illegal block because the blocker (No. 78) has contacted his opponent above the shoulders. When the defensive player (No. 87), by trying to duck or submarine under the blocker, is responsible for the "high" block, no penalty is called against the blocker.

33

TACKLING

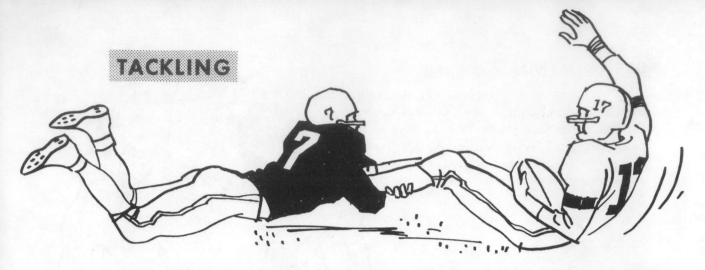

The defender (No. 7) is making the standard two-armed tackle to bring the runner (No. 17) down. As soon as any part of the runner's body, except his hands and feet, touches the ground, he is not permitted to make any further advance. In High School and College rules a runner is "down" whether he has touched the ground because of a tackle or simply through slipping or falling. In Professional football, when a runner slips or falls he is not considered "down" and may continue to advance the ball until he is tackled.

This may not be the classic way to make a tackle, but it is *legal to grab the runner* around the neck or any part of his body. The tackler, however, has to be sure that he is not grabbing the runner's face mask.

A push in time may stop a long gain and the defender (No. 88) is within the rules when he pushes the runner (No. 25) to the ground. The defense is allowed to use hands and arms to tackle, push, shove or otherwise *throw the runner* to the ground.

LEGAL USE OF HANDS

The defender (No. 78) is using his hands in a legal manner to push the blocker and pursue the runner. A *defensive player* is allowed to use his hands and arms to grasp, push, pull or lift other offensive players out of his way if he is trying to reach the runner.

DISQUALIFYING FOUL

The defensive player (No. 70) will be disqualified for *punching* his opponent (No. 15) and his team will be penalized 15 yards. The rule forbids any player from striking another with his fist, forearm, elbow or locked hands, or to kick or knee an opponent. The *disqualifying foul* rule differs from the *personal foul* rule in that the action is considered by the officials to be performed deliberately and willfully with intent to harm.

PERSONAL FOULS

KNEEING

The blocker (No. 76) is guilty of *kneeing* his opponent (No. 15) and is penalized 15 yards since it is not considered a deliberate act. Under the same rule no player shall hit an opponent either on the head, neck or face with the heel, back or side of the hand or with the wrist.

ACCIDENTAL KICK

No. 47 has *inadvertently kicked* an opposing player on the ground while trying to reach the runner. He will be penalized 15 yards under the rule that prohibits any player from swinging his foot and striking another player above the knee with his foot.

TRIPPING

The runner (No. 12) is being tripped by the defensive player (No. 17) and the infraction will cost the team on defense 15 yards *Tripping* is never allowed, regardless of whether the tripped player is carrying the ball or not.

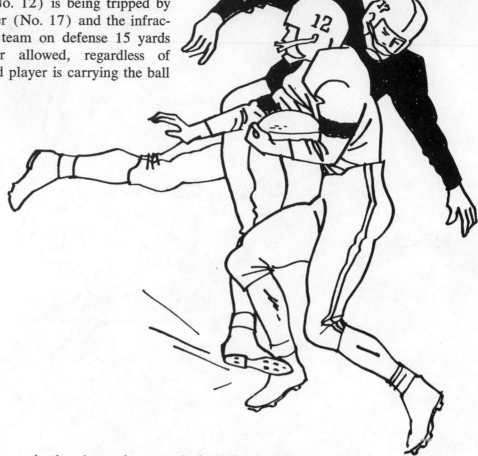

PILINC ON

Since the runner is already on the ground, the defensive player (No. 19) who is about to fall on him will be guilty of *piling on* and will be penalized 15 yards. Once the ball becomes dead players are expected to stop running into or throwing themselves on an opponent.

Any hurdling by the runner (No. 11) is best left for the track event. He will be penalized 15 yards for jumping over an opponent at the scrimmage line.

When the runner (No. 12) is obviously out of bounds, no defensive player may tackle him. The penalty is 15 yards.

CLIPPING

The block being performed on No. 69 is called *clipping* and, contrary to popular belief, it is *not necessarily illegal.* Clipping means a player has thrown himself across the back of the legs or the back of an opponent other than the runner. In a scrimmage play clipping is permitted in an area about 6 yards in depth and 4 yards wide on each side of the middle lineman. But any offensive player outside this area who is in motion toward the ball when it is snapped may not clip in this area. During a kick-off, or other free-kick down, no clipping is permitted. The penalty is 15 yards.

The referee has already taken possession of the ball, making it clear the play is over. The illegal tackle will draw a 15-yard penalty under the rule that bars any player from running into or making contact with an opponent obviously out of the play either before or after the ball is dead.

The face mask or protector is off-limits and grabbing a player's mask is forbidden. The penalty is 15 yards.

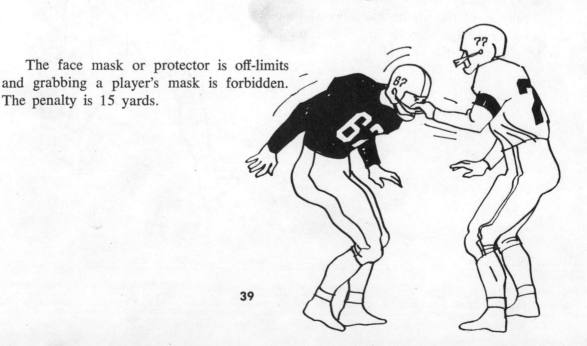

39

FORWARD PASS

ILLEGAL PASS

The passer (No. 21) has gone one step too far before throwing the ball because his left foot has *crossed the neutral zone*. It is is 5 yards from the spot of the pass and the down counts.

LEGAL PASS

The passer is now able to throw the ball legally even though he has stepped past his own scrimmage line. He has been careful not to go beyond the neutral zone.

INTENTIONAL GROUNDING

The passer will be penalized for throwing the ball away to prevent loss of yardage. He is about to be tackled and brought down. Since there is no receiver reasonably near the area, the passer is guilty of *intentionally grounding the pass*. The penalty is loss of 5 yards and a down.

JUDGMENT CALL

This passing situation is more complicated. The passer, No. 11, throws the ball in the general direction of the receiver just as he is about to be tackled. The question that the referee has to settle is whether it was a bona-fide attempt at completing a pass or whether it was a clever attempt to prevent a loss on the play. This is a judgment call and, unless the evidence is overwhelming on the other side, the official will rule it a legal forward pass.

41

ELIGIBLE RECEIVERS

The arrows point to the only players on the offensive team who are eligible pass receivers: the two ends on the scrimmage line and the players in the backfield who are at least 1 yard in back of the scrimmage line. In Professional football, the T quarterback is not an eligible receiver. The rule on eligible receivers remains the same regardless of whether the end man is a tackle or guard in another formation. All 11 players on the defensive team are eligible to intercept a pass.

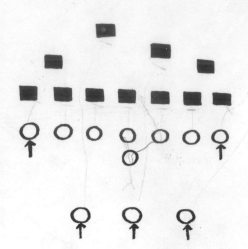

STEPPING OUT-OF-BOUNDS

In the illustration at the left, an otherwise eligible receiver has made himself ineligible by going out-of-bounds before returning to the field to catch a pass. On the right, the ineligible receiver becomes eligible because the pass has been touched by a defensive player.

LANDING OUT-OF-BOUNDS

The receiver, No. 21, made a nice catch of the forward pass, but the effort was wasted. Though he is inbounds when he leaped for the ball, he landed outside the sideline. In such a situation the receiver is ruled out-of-bounds and the pass is incomplete.

PRETENDED FUMBLE

The runner, No. 19, is attempting to execute a clever maneuver by throwing the ball forward, pretending to fumble so that teammate No. 77 will recover the ball for additional yardage. But any attempt to throw the ball forward beyond the neutral zone is classified as an illegal forward pass and will be penalized 5 yards from that point.

SIMULTANEOUS CATCH

In this example "half a loaf" is about as good as a whole one. The intended receiver (No. 89) and the defender (No. 21) caught the pass simultaneously. It will be ruled a completed pass and the ball given to the passing team. There is a limitation in such a situation: the receiver may not advance the ball.

44

The passing team may appear to be lucky because the football has bounced off the helmet of one of its players (No. 68) into the hands of another. But it will not be ruled a completed forward pass because the ball, even if only accidentally, touched an ineligible receiver first.

JUDGMENT CALL

The receiver caught the forward pass, or did he? He has possession of the ball momentarily. It slipped through his hands just as he was about to take his first step. *The judgment of the nearest official* will determine whether the receiver actually had possession of the ball or whether the ruling should be an incomplete pass.

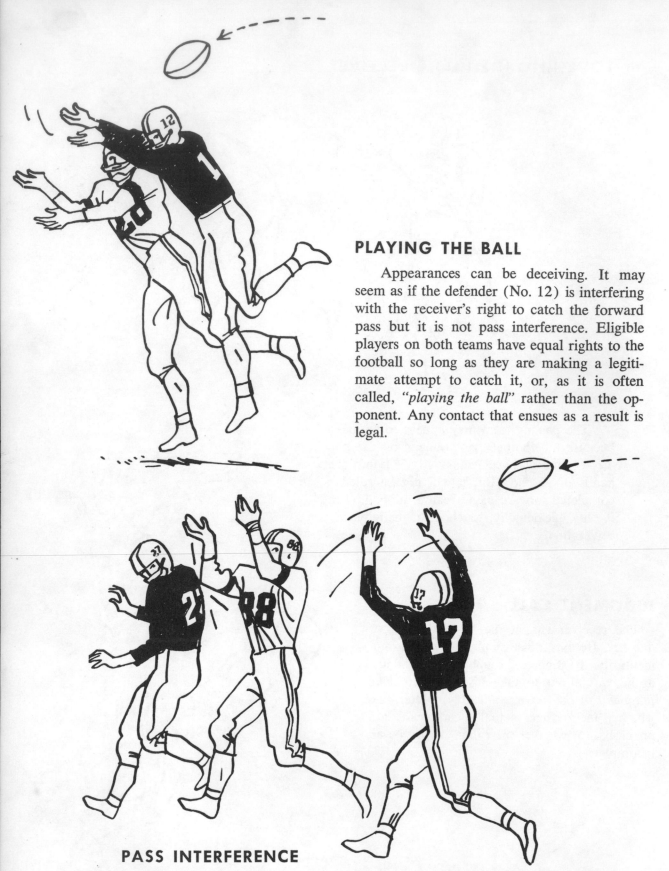

PLAYING THE BALL

Appearances can be deceiving. It may seem as if the defender (No. 12) is interfering with the receiver's right to catch the forward pass but it is not pass interference. Eligible players on both teams have equal rights to the football so long as they are making a legitimate attempt to catch it, or, as it is often called, *"playing the ball"* rather than the opponent. Any contact that ensues as a result is legal.

PASS INTERFERENCE

This is pass interference even though the offender (No. 17) has not made contact with the receiver (No. 88). No. 17 is attempting to distract the receiver from catching the pass by waving his arms in front of him. With his back to the play, the defender is not making an honest effort to "play the ball." Under the rule it is the passing team's ball at the spot of the foul.

BEFORE THE PASS IS THROWN

The defender (No. 17) is not guilty of pass interference because contact with the receiver (No. 89) was made before the ball was thrown and was beyond the scrimmage line.

INELIGIBLE RECEIVER DOWNFIELD

Offensive guard (No. 69), having completed his primary block on the opposing defensive player, is running downfield to assist with the blocking for the intended receiver. He is, however, committing an infraction of the rules: once he has lost contact with his opponent he cannot make a move downfield until the pass is thrown. He is not an eligible receiver and should not be downfield. The team will be penalized 15 yards for having an ineligible receiver downfield.

PASS INTERFERENCE RULE

Even though the pass thrown by No. 17 has not yet crossed the scrimmage line, pass interference rules are in effect. The rules apply from *the moment the pass is thrown*. The defensive player (No. 25) is guilty of interfering with the intended pass receiver (No. 89) and the penalty will give the passing team a first down at the spot where the interference occurred.

ALMOST A SAFETY

The defensive player (No. 78) has almost scored 2 points for his team by batting back a forward pass thrown from the end zone. If he had been *inside the end zone* instead of a few yards out when he batted back the pass, he would have been credited with a safety.

DEAD BALL

The *ball is ruled dead* the instant a forward pass hits a goal post, even though it may bounce off and be caught by a player before it touches the ground. The rules state that the ball is dead upon hitting the goal posts, the crossbar, the ground or going out of bounds.

FUMBLE ON A PASS PLAY

The passer (No. 12) has fumbled the ball in attempting to pass it forward to an eligible receiver (No. 27) behind the scrimmage line. It is ruled a fumble and not an incomplete pass. The importance of this is that now the defensive team can recover the ball. If it were an incomplete pass the passing team would automatically retain possession of the ball.

INTERCEPTION

The pass has touched an ineligible receiver and the defender (No. 89) is about to intercept. The ruling is that *the interception stands* unless the defensive team prefers to take the penalty. A forward pass remains in play *only for an interception after touching an ineligible receiver*. In Professional football there is a penalty for intentional touching, none for accidental.

SCHOOL AND PRO RULE

Two *eligible receivers* have caught the pass simultaneously. In High School and College it is ruled a completed pass, but among the Professionals it is ruled incomplete.

BATTING BALL ON A PASS PLAY

The defender (No. 21) bats the attempted forward pass away from the intended receiver (No. 27). Under the rule the *defense* is allowed to bat the pass in any direction and at any time but the *offense* is allowed only to bat the ball to prevent an interception.

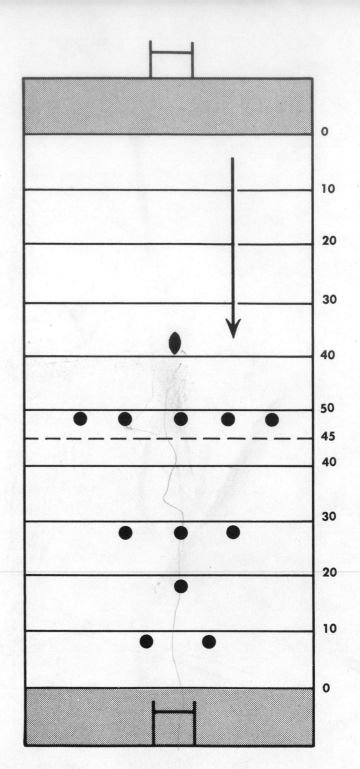

KICK-OFF FORMATION

Five players of the *team receiving* the kick-off must be in an area 10 to 15 yards from the kick-off, between the 50-yard line and their own 45-yard line. There are no restrictions on where the other players are located, except that they must be in back of the first five players.

56

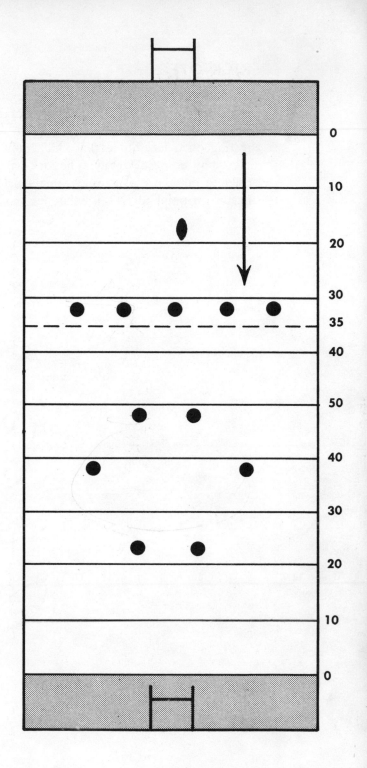

FREE-KICK FORMATION

The free kick follows a safety. Five players of the *team receiving* the kick must be in an area 10 to 15 yards from the ball, between the 30-yard line and the 35-yard line.

KICK-OFF

The ball is put into play at the start of each half by the *kick-off*. The ball is placed on the 40-yard line of the kicking team, usually resting on a tee, but a place-kick or a drop-kick may be used legally. The kick-off is also used to put the ball in play after a field goal or try-for-point after a touchdown.

PUNT

The punt is usually used on a scrimmage play. The ball is kicked before it touches the ground. It may also be used as a free-kick after a safety. Team punting gives up possession of the ball.

58

PLACE-KICK

The ball is held for the kicker by a teammate. The place-kick is used to score a field-goal, point-after-touchdown, and sometimes on a kick-off.

DROP-KICK

The kicker drops the ball and kicks it just at the instant it touches the ground or a fraction of a second later. Seldom employed today, it can be used instead of the place-kick.

ILLEGALLY KICKING THE BALL

The ball may not be kicked by any player except during a specific kicking play. Since the defensive player (No. 12) has deliberately kicked a free ball, the offensive team has possession of the ball at the spot where the rule infraction occurred. If the player on offense kicks the ball, his team is given a 15-yard penalty from the starting point of the play.

60

ROUGHING THE KICKER

After the punter (No. 27) kicks the ball, an opposing player crashes into him: a clear violation of roughing-the-kicker regulations. The purpose of the rule is to protect the kicker and the holder of a place-kick during a scrimmage kick because they are vulnerable to contact. To gain protection under the rules, it has to be reasonably obvious that a kick will be made. Penalty for roughing the kicker is 15 yards.

ON A BLOCKED PUNT

A roughing-the-kicker penalty will not be called on this play because *the punt has been blocked*. Such contact is considered a legitimate play when the punt is blocked. The defensive player (No. 77), therefore, is not violating any rules by running into the kicker.

SLIGHT CONTACT

When the contact is slight, the defensive player (No. 77) will not be called for roughing the kicker.

ON THE QUICK KICK

Since a *quick kick* was attempted, the defensive player (No. 70) is exempt from the roughing-the-kicker rule because it was not reasonably obvious that a scrimmage kick was planned. No penalty.

FUMBLE ON KICKING PLAY   A fumble before the kick is attempted also exempts

the defensive players from the roughing-the-kicker rule.

FAIR CATCH

WRONG

RIGHT

FAIR CATCH SIGNAL

If the signal for a *fair catch* is given improperly, the receiving team is penalized 15 yards from the spot of the foul. On the left, the wrong way to signal; on the right, the player gives the proper signal.

PROTECTING PUNT RECEIVER

The players crowd about the man catching the ball but they have to be careful to give him an *unmolested opportunity* to catch it. If they interfere, the penalty is 15 yards.

ILLEGAL INTERFERENCE ON A CATCH

Even though he manages to catch the ball as he is being tackled, his team will be awarded a 15-yard penalty. Under the rule, illegal interference is called when a player is tackled before or when the ball arrives.

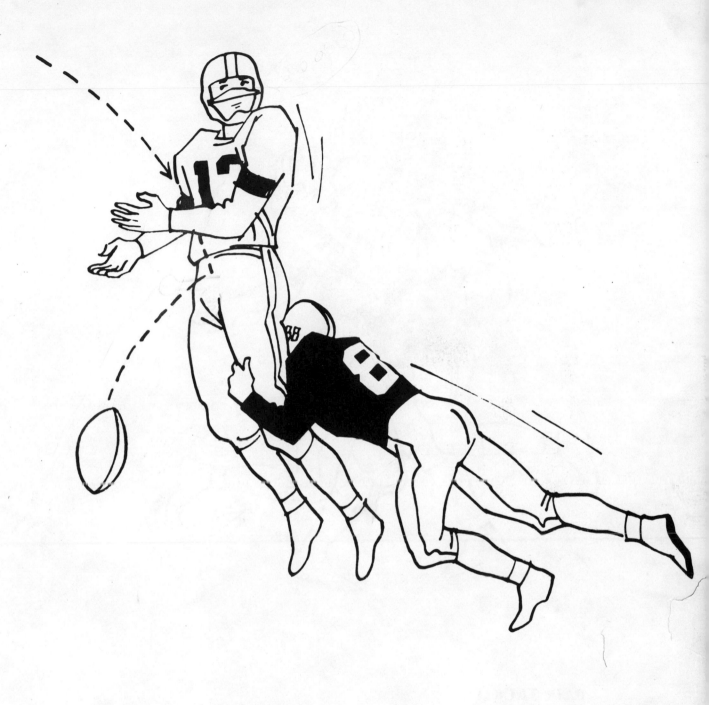

NO FUMBLE ON CATCH

Although the receiver of the punt fumbled while he was being tackled, the official will rule no fumble. His opponent will be penalized 15 yards. The receiving team will retain possession of the ball because of the illegal interference.

FAIR TACKLE

The receiver of the punt has fumbled and then is tackled by an opponent. No interference will be called. Protection against interference with the opportunity to catch a kick ends when the player *touches the ball,* except when it is a fair catch.

1   2

TWO-STEP LIMIT

After making a fair catch, a player is allowed to take only two steps. The ball becomes dead at the spot where he caught it. If he tries to advance, he will be penalized 5 yards.

OFFICIAL'S CODE OF SIGNALS

OFFSIDE. A player on either team has crossed his scrimmage line before the ball has been snapped (put into play). Penalty: 5 yards.

ILLEGAL RETURN. Return of a substitute previously disqualified, or before a down has been completed (College). Penalty: 15 yards.

CLIPPING. A foul committed when a player attempts to block from behind by throwing himself across the back or legs of an opposing player other than the runner. Penalty: 15 yards.

ILLEGAL PROCEDURE. This indicates several different infractions, the more common being: false start; having less than 7 players on the offensive team's scrimmage line; illegally handing the ball forward; taking more than 2 steps after a fair catch; illegal snap; infraction of substitution rules (College); invalid fair-catch signal (Professional).

DELAY OF GAME. Excess time-outs requested or used; illegal delay of game; crawling (High School and College); team not ready to play (College penalty: 15 yards); illegal substitution (High School); interference with opponent or snap of the ball (High School). Penalty: 5 yards.

ROUGHING-THE-KICKER. The kicker, or the holder of the ball for the place-kick, has been run into or otherwise illegally interfered with. Penalty: 15 yards.

ILLEGAL MOTION. Player or players illegally in motion when the ball is snapped. Penalty: 5 yards.

PERSONAL FOUL. Piling on; hurdling; tripping; tackling out-of-bounds; running into opponent obviously out of play; striking; kicking or kneeing an opponent; tackling player who signalled for fair catch; grabbing the face mask of opponent (College).

UNSPORTSMANLIKE CONDUCT. Besides general unsportsmanlike conduct by player or coach, the signal also indicates: persons illegally on the field; delaying start of either half (High School); invalid signal for a fair catch (College). Penalty: 15 yards.

ILLEGAL SHIFT. Player or players failed to stop for one second after a shift. Penalty: 5 yards.

PERSONAL FOUL. In Professional football, the referee will give an additional signal to define more precisely the rule infraction.

ILLEGAL USE OF HANDS. Penalty: 15 yards.

INTENTIONAL GROUNDING OF PASS. Penalty: 5 yards and loss of down.

INCOMPLETE FORWARD PASS. The signal also indicates a penalty has been refused; a field-goal or point-after-touchdown kick has been missed.

TIME-OUT. In High School and College games, if the official calls for time-out on his own, he taps his chest; in Professional football, the official places one hand on his cap.

ILLEGALLY PASSING OR HANDING THE BALL FORWARD. Penalty: 5 yards and loss of down.

INTERLOCKED INTERFERENCE, OR HELPING THE RUNNER. Penalty: 15 yards. In Professional football only, crawling: 5-yard penalty.

PASS OR KICK INTERFERENCE. Offensive pass interference: 15-yard penalty. Defensive pass interference: Pass ruled completed at spot of foul. Interference with fair-catch opportunity: 15-yard penalty.

BALL IS DEAD.

FIRST DOWN. The team in possession of the ball has a first down and now has four downs (plays) in which to gain 10 yards for another first down.

ILLEGAL RECEIVER DOWNFIELD. Penalty: 15 yards.

SCORE. Touchdown, field goal, or place-kick has been made.

BALL IS READY FOR PLAY.

ILLEGALLY KICKING, BATTING, OR TOUCHING BALL. Illegal kick: 5-yard penalty; illegally kicking ball: 15-yard penalty; illegally kicking or batting free ball: College rules give the offended team possession of the ball at the spot where foul was committed; High School rules call for a 15-yard penalty; forward pass illegally touched: College rules provide for 5 or 15 yards penalty and/or loss of down.

SAFETY.

GAME CLOCK STARTS.

OFFICIAL NFL
DIGEST OF RULES

FIELD

1. Side lines and end lines are out of bounds. Goal line is actually in the end zone.
2. The four intersections of goal lines and side lines must be marked, at INSIDE corners (field of play) by flags mounted on flexible shafts.
3. Inbound lines (hash marks) are 20 yards in from each side line.
4. Goal posts—18 feet 6 inches wide and top face of crossbar 10 feet above ground. Vertical goal posts extend 20 feet above crossbar. The goal is the vertical plane extending indefinitely above crossbar and between the lines indicated by the *outer edges* of the goal posts.
5. The playing field will be rimmed by a white border 6 feet wide along the sideline.

COIN TOSS

1. Toss of coin will take place thirty minutes before scheduled game time in center of field.
   (a) Toss will be called by visiting team captain.
   (b) The winner of toss must choose one of two privileges, and the loser is given the other. The two choices are:
      1. Which team is to kick-off
      2. The goal his team is to defend
   (c) At the end of first half, the captains of both teams must immediately appear at center of field in order to inform Referee of their respective choices.
2. In case of inclement weather, toss may be made between the two coaches.
3. Three minutes prior to game time, both captains are to appear at center of field at which time Referee will indicate which team is to kick-off, and goal receivers will defend. No toss simulated.

TIMING

1. NFL official game time is kept on stadium clock by a timer trained by the NFL office.
2. Two minutes intermission between periods and team time outs, timed by the Field Judge.
3. Offensive team has thirty seconds to put ball in play. Timed by Field Judge, and failure to do so is delay of game. Penalty 5 yards.

TIMING CHANGES DURING LAST
TWO MINUTES OF EACH HALF

1. On kick-off clock does not start until the ball has been legally touched by a player of either team in the field of play.
2. During the last two minutes a team cannot buy a fourth time out for a penalty. A fourth time out during the last two minutes will only be allowed for an injured player who must be immediately designated and removed. No penalty. Fifth or more are allowed only under the same condition, but are penalized 5 yards. (Time in with Referee's ready signal in both cases)
3. During last two minutes of either half, if score is tied or team in possession is behind in score and has exhausted its legal time outs, an additional time out may be requested and granted under the same conditions as above. Clock shall start with Referee's whistle upon removal of injured player from field, and ball cannot be put in play until ten seconds have expired. Game can end before snap if less than ten seconds remain.

TRY FOR POINT

1. NFL teams, after scoring a touchdown, may try for one additional point by kicking a legal field goal (try-kick).

SUBSTITUTIONS

1. Unlimited substitution. Players may enter the field only when ball is dead.
2. Players leaving field must clear field on their own side, *between end lines* before snap or free-kick. If player crosses end line leaving field, 5-yard penalty for delay of game.

KICK-OFF (FREE-KICK)

1. Start of game, start of second half, after a field goal and following a try for point.
   (a) On the above situations a 3-inch kicking "T" may be used. Punt not allowed. Kick must be made from on or between inbounds lines.
2. Kick-off is not a legal kick unless kick travels 10 yards or has been touched by receivers. Once ball touched by receiving team it is a free ball. Receivers may recover and advance, kicking team may recover, but not advance, unless receivers had possession of ball.
3. A kick-off which goes out of bounds between the goal lines without being touched by receiving team, must be re-kicked. (5-yard penalty) If touched last by receiving team it is their ball at inbound spot. The last touching is the important thing even though it may have been touched by both teams.
4. Free-kick situations also develop following fair catch and safety. Time starts with Referee's whistle.

When receiving team fair catches ball, captain has option on how he wishes to put ball in play. (1) Free-kick (punt, drop-kick, or place-kick without "T") or (2) By snap. If place or drop-kick attempted and ball kicked between uprights, field goal is awarded for successful kick. (3 points) All other free-kick rules apply.

Following a safety the team scored upon must next put ball in play at their 20-yard line by free-kick. (Punt, drop-kick or place-kick—no "T") All free-kick rules apply. No score may be made on free-kick following safety, even though a series of penalties may place a team in position to do so.

SAFETY

1. A safety is the situation in which ball is dead on or behind a team's goal line. Provided: The impetus came from a player of that team. (2 points)

Examples:
   (a) Blocked punt which goes out of the kicking team's end zone. Impetus was put on ball by the punting team; the block only changes direction of ball and not the impetus. (2 points)
   (b) Ball carrier runs into his own end zone and is downed. Ball carrier responsible for ball being in the end zone. (2 points)
   (c) Safety by penalty: When offensive team commits a foul, and spot of enforcement is behind their goal line. (2 points)
2. Player intercepts a pass in his own end zone and is downed. TOUCHBACK—Impetus came from forward pass.
3. If the intercepting momentum of a pass interception, inside intercepting teams' 5-yard line, carries the interceptor and the ball into the end zone, the ball is next in play at spot of interception, unless the intercepting player advances into field of play. This is irrespective of any other act (muff, fumble, pass or recovery) by either offensive or defensive team.

POSITION OF PLAYERS AT SNAP

1. Offensive team must have seven or more players on the line of scrimmage at snap.
2. Offensive players, other than the snap receiver who are not on line of scrimmage, must be at least one yard behind line at snap.
3. After neutral zone starts, no player of either team may encroach upon it, nor may he be off-side at snap.
4. From start of neutral zone until snap, no offensive player after assuming a set position shall charge or move in such a way as to lead defense to believe that the snap has started.
5. A player entering game wearing an illegal number for the position he takes, must report to the Referee. Referee in turn will report same to the defensive captain. (Specifically, player wearing ineligible pass receiver number, playing eligible pass receiving position)
6. After a huddle or shift all plapers of offensive team, after assuming a set position, must come to an absolute stop. Players must remain stationary for a period of at least one second before snap. There shall be no movement of feet, head, arms or swaying of body. (5-yard penalty for illegal pause or motion)
7. Lineman may lock legs with the snapper only.

USE OF HANDS, ARMS AND BODY

1. No player on offense may assist runner except by individually blocking opponents for him, and there shall be no interlocked interference.
2. Interior lineman who takes or simulates a three point stance must not move before snap. (5-yard penalty—false start)
3. Runner may ward off opponents with his hands and arms, but no other offensive player may use them to obstruct an opponent. That is, grasping with hands or using them to push, encircling with arm in any degree any part of body, during block.
4. A defensive player may not tackle or hold any opponent other than a runner. He may use his hands and arms only:
    (1) To ward off an obstructing opponent
    (2) To push or pull him out of the way on line or scrimmage or to cross it
    (3) In an actual attempt to get at or tackle runner
    (4) To push or pull him out of the way in an actual legal attempt to recover a loose ball
    (5) During a legal block

5. A defensive player shall not contact an opponent above shoulders with palm of his hands except during an initial charge or to ward him off on line, and then only if it is not a repeated act against the same opponent during any one contact. Otherwise they may be used on his head, neck, or face only to ward off or push him in an actual legal attempt to get at ball.
6. Any offensive player who pretends to possess the ball, and/or one to whom a teammate pretends to give the ball, may be tackled provided he is *crossing* his scrimmage line between the offensive ends of a normal tight offensive line.
7. A player of either team may block any time provided it is not pass interference, fair catch interference, or otherwise unnecessary roughness.
8. A player may not bat or punch:
    (a) A loose ball (in field of play) towards opponents' goal line, or in any direction if it is in either end zone.
    (b) A ball in player possession or attempt to do so.
    Exception: A pass in flight (forward or backward) may be batted in any direction, or at any time (including end zone), by (a) defense and (b) offense only to prevent an opponent from intercepting. (Penalty for illegal batting or punching of ball: loss of 15 yards)
9. No player may kick or kick at any ball except as a punt, drop-kick, or place-kick. (Illegal kicking with foot, loss of 15 yards)

FORWARD PASS

1. Offensive team may make only one forward pass during each play from scrimmage. Penalty for second pass behind the line of scrimmage is loss of down from previous spot.
2. Forward pass from beyond line of scrimmage. Penalty, loss of down and 5 yards—enforced from the spot of the pass.
3. Forward pass from behind the line of scrimmage may be caught by only only eligible offensive receiver. All players on defense are eligible. If forward pass is touched by a defensive man, all players on the offensive team become eligible.
4. If a pass is caught simultaneously by two eligible *opposing* players, ball is awarded to passing team.
5. Any forward pass legal or illegal) becomes incomplete and ball is dead immediately if pass:
    (a) Strikes ground or goes out of bounds.
    (b) Strikes goal post or crossbar of either team.
    (c) Is caught by any offensive player after it has touched an ineligible receiver, or second eligible receiver, and before any touching by defense.
    (d) When illegal pass is caught by the passers.
6. A pass is complete when receiver touches the ground with *both* feet inbounds and with the ball in his possession. If a receiver is carried out of bounds by an opponent, while he is in possession inbounds in the air, pass is complete at out-of-bounds spot.
7. If a pass is touched by any ineligible receiver on or behind line or touches him beyond line, it is loss of down and 15 yards. (Before any touching by defense)
8. Fourth down pass—when offensive team is inside opponents' 20-yard line and fourth down pass is incomplete in end zone,

it is an automatic touchback. Opponents' ball first and ten on 20-yard line.

9. (a) Ineligible receiver downfield. (Penalty is 15 yards.)
   (b) Pass touched by ineligible receiver that has not been touched by a defensive man, is a foul. (Loss of down *and* 15 yards.)
10. Personal foul committed by the *defense prior* to the completion of a pass. (Penalty—15 yards added on to spot where ball becomes dead.)
11. Personal foul committed by the *offense prior* to the completion of a pass. (Penalty—15 yards from previous spot (line of scrimmage) *unless* foul was behind that spot.)

INTENTIONAL GROUNDING OF A PASS

Under the following conditions, it is considered intentional grounding:

1. No eligible pass receivers in position to catch ball.
2. No defensive players in position to catch the ball.
3. Deliberate attempt to prevent the loss of yards by his team.
4. When the ball is deliberately thrown out of bounds or out of the end zone with any of the conditions outlined under 1, 2, and 3. (Penalty 15 yards and loss of down.)

PASS INTERFERENCE

1. The restriction for the passing team starts with the snap of the ball, and the restriction for the defensive team starts when the ball leaves the passer's hand, and ends when the ball is touched by anyone.
2. Defensive pass interference. (Penalty—automatic first down at the spot of foul.)
3. Offensive pass interference including ineligible receiver downfield. (Penalty—15 yards from previous spot.)
4. It is interference by either offense or defense when any player movement beyond offensive team's line hinders the progress of an eligible opponent in his attempt to reach pass, except such incidental movement or contact which may occur when two or more eligible players make a simultaneous and bona fide attempt to catch or bat ball. This restriction ends for both teams when pass is touched.
5. "Simultaneous and bona fide" has reference to and shall be taken to mean the coming together of opposing eligible receivers at spot of possible completion or interception of a pass, when each of the players is intent on "playing the ball" and where contact between the players is unavoidable and incidental to the act or effort involved in attempting to catch or bat ball. Any contact prior to such a time is interference by either one or both players.
6. During a forward pass, it must be remembered that defensive players have as much right to the *path to ball* as eligible opponents. Any bodily contact, however severe, between players who are making a bona fide and simultaneous attempt to catch or bat ball, is not interference.
7. Pass interference by defense is independent of the direction in flight of pass, and as to whether or not offensive team might have completed it. This is not a judgment situation on the part of the official. Passer may have changed his pass to another receiver due to interference or a possible receiver being covered.

BACKWARD PASS—FUMBLE

1. Fumble may be advanced by anyone, offense or defense.
2. Backward pass. (lateral pass)
   (a) Offensive team may advance a fumbled lateral.
   (b) Defensive team may only gain possession, unless caught in the air.
3. Fourth down fumble on or inside defensive team's 10-yard line (during play from scrimmage) before any touching by defensive team, only the offensive player fumbling the ball may advance it. If recovered or advanced by any other offensive player, the ball is dead at the spot of the fumble unless spot of recovery is behind the spot of the fumble.

PUNT

1. Any punt or attempted field goal that touches the receiver's end zone or goal post is dead. Automatic touchback.

2. Any punt that touches kicker's goal post, ball continues in play. In such cases all rules pertaining to a scrimmage kick continue in force until kick ends.
3. Any punt that is blocked and does not cross the line of scrimmage is not a kicked ball—both teams eligible to recover and advance. Yardage to be gained must be made for first down.
4. Kicking team may never advance its own kick even though legal recovery was made. Possession only.
5. A member of the kicking team cannot down the ball on or inside opponent's 5-yard line if his momentum carries the ball into end zone. Possible to down ball on 1-inch line providing ball does not touch anything in end zone.
6. Fouls during a punt are enforced from the previous spot—line of scrimmage, unless by offensive team behind line of scrimmage. (Exceptions: Illegal touching, illegal fair catch interference, invalid fair catch signal and foul by kickers behind the line of scrimmage.) A punted ball remains a kicked ball until possessed by a player of either team or is declared dead.
7. Any member of the punting team may down the ball anywhere in the field of play. Illegal touching rule applies. For illegally touching a scrimmage kick: Official's time out and receiver's ball at any spot of illegal touching or possession. This foul does not offset a foul by the receivers during the down.

FAIR CATCH

1. Valid only when one arm raised full lngth above the head.
2. Applies to all members of the receiving team. However, they are *not required* to catch the ball.
3. If a player signals (valid or invalid) for a fair catch, he may not block or initiate contact with one of the kickers until the ball touches a player.
   PENALTY: For unsportsmanlike conduct after fair catch signal: Snap by receivers 15 yards behind spot of foul.
4. If ball hits ground or touches one of the kicking team in flight, fair catch signal is off, and all rules for a kicked ball apply.
5. Interference with the opportunity to make a fair catch, 15-yard penalty. Any undue advance by a fair catch receiver is delay of the game. (5-yard penalty)
6. If time expires while ball is in play and a fair catch has been awarded to a team, they may choose to extend period by one free-kick down.

FOUL ON LAST PLAY OF HALF OR GAME

1. Foul by defense on last play of half or game: Down will be replayed if penalty is accepted.
2. Foul by offense on last play of half or game: Down will not be replayed, and the play in which the foul is committed is nullified. (No extension of period for an offensive foul)
   Exception: Fair catch interference, illegal touching. No score by offense is counted.
3. Double foul on last play of half or game: The down is replayed.

DEFINITIONS

1. *BALL IN PLAY:* Ball is in play when it is legally free-kicked or snapped. It continues in play until down ends.
2. *DEAD BALL:* A dead ball is one which is not in play. The time period during which ball is dead is between downs.
3. *LOOSE BALL:* A loose ball is a live ball which is not in player possession.
4. *MUFF:* A muff is the touching of ball by a player in an unsuccessful attempt to obtain possession of a loose ball.
5. *POSSESSION:* A player is in possession when he has held ball long enough to give him such control as to enable him to perform any act common to game.
6. *FOUL AND SPOT OF ENFORCEMENT:* A foul is any violation of a playing rule. Spot of enforcement (basic spot) is the spot at which a penalty for a foul is enforced. Four such spots are commonly used.
   (a) Spot of Foul—Spot where foul was commited or is so considered by rule.
   (b) Previous Spot—Spot where ball was last put in play.
   (c) Spot of Snap, Pass, Fumble, Return Kick or Free-Kick—

Spot where the act connected with a given foul occurred or at which penalty is to be enforced.

(d) Succeeding Spot—Spot where ball would next be put in play if no distance penalty were to be enforced.
Exception: If foul occurs after a touchdown and before the whistle for a try, succeeding spot is spot of next kick-off.

7. *FREE-KICK:* A free-kick is one which puts ball in play to start a free-kick down. It includes kick-off, safety-kick, and fair-catch kick.

8. *IMPETUS:* Impetus is the action of a player which gives momentum to ball.

9. *NEUTRAL ZONE:* The neutral zone is the space length of ball between the offensive and defensive teams.

10. *ENCROACHING:* A player is encroaching on the neutral zone when any part of his body is in the neutral zone.
Exception: The snapper is not considered in the neutral zone if no part of his body *is beyond* defensive team line. (Forward point of ball)

11. *SHIFT:* A shift is the action of two or more offensive players who (prior to a snap) after having assumed a set position, simultaneously change the position of their feet by pivoting to, or assuming a new set position with either one foot or both feet.

12. *SAFETY:* A safety is the situation in which ball is dead on or behind a team's own goal line, provided: The impetus came from a player of that team.

13. *TOUCHBACK:* A touchback is the situation in which a ball is dead on or behind a team's own goal line, provided: The impetus came from an opponent and provided it is not a touchdown.

FOULS

1. *ENCROACHMENT:* Example: Defensive lineman moving across the neutral zone and making contact with an opponent prior to the ball being snapped. Whistle kills play. No snap allowed.

2. *OFF-SIDES:* A player is off-sides when any part of his person is beyond his line of scrimmage, or free-kick line, when the ball is put into play. (Does not include offensive center when he is snapping ball)

3. *RUNNING INTO PASSER:* Penalty: Loss of 15 yards from previous spot, and disqualification when flagrant.
Note: The Rules Committee is definitely committed to the policy of protecting the passer. A passer who is standing still or fading backwards, is obviously out of the play after ball has left his hand or hands, and is to be protected until pass ends, or until he starts to move into a distinctly defensive position. Referee must determine whether opponent had a reasonable chance to stop his momentum during an attempt to block or bat pass, or to tackle passer while he was still in possession.

4. *RUNNING INTO KICKER:* Penalty: For running into kicker, loss of 5 yards from previous spot. For roughness, 15 yards, and disqualification when flagrant. (1st down in either case)
Note: Avoiding the kicker is a primary responsibility of defensive players if they do not touch the kick. A defensive player may touch a kicker only if he has previously touched the ball, or if the contact is caused by the kicker.

5. *AUTOMATIC FIRST DOWN:* Offensive team will be awarded first down on all defensive fouls with these five exceptions:
(a) Off-sides
(b) Encroachment
(c) Delay of game
(d) Illegal substitution
(e) Excessive time outs

PENALTY ENFORCED ON FOLLOWING KICK-OFF

1. A team scores (touchdown, field goal, extra point or safety), and opponents commit a personal foul, unsportsmanlike conduct foul or obviously unfair act during the down—Penalty will be assessed on the following kick-off.

2. During continuing action after a team scores, if either team commits a personal foul—Penalty will be assessed on the following kick-off.

SUMMARY OF PENALTIES

FIVE YARDS

1. Crawling, pushing or helping runner.
2. Defensive holding. (automatic first down)
3. Delay of game.
4. Encroachment.
5. Exceeding thirty-second period.
6. Excessive time outs.
7. False start.
8. Illegal formation. (player neither on nor off the line of scrimmage at snap)
9. Illegal double shift.
10. Illegal motion.
11. Illegal motion by interior linemen.
12. Illegal substitution.
13. Kick-off out of bounds between goal lines without being touched by any player.
14. Making a forward pass beyond the line of scrimmage. (also loss of down)
15. Making an invalid fair catch signal.
16. More than eleven players on field during play.
17. Offensive team having less than seven men on the line of scrimmage at snap.
18. Off-sides.
19. Pausing less than one second after huddle or shift.
20. Running into kicker.
21. Short free-kick.
22. Two or more players in motion at snap.

FIFTEEN YARDS

1. Clipping.
2. Fair catch interference.
3. Forward pass intentionally touched by an ineligible receiver. (also loss of down)
4. Grabbing face mask of any player. (if by defense, automatic first down)
5. Illegal batting, kicking or punching a loose ball. (if by defense, automatic first down)
6. Illegal use of hands and arms on offense.
7. Ineligible receiver down field.
8. Intentionally grounding the ball. (also loss of down)
9. Offensive pass interference.
10. Piling on. (if by defense, automatic first down)
11. Roughing the kicker. (automatic first down)
12. Roughing the passer. (automatic first down)
13. Unnecessary roughness. (if by defense, automatic first down)
14. Unsportsmanlike conduct. Player may not shove, push, strike or lay a hand on an official in an offensive or visual manner which may be misinterpreted.

BALL PLACED ON ONE YARD LINE

1. Defensive pass interference in defensive team's end zone. Offensive team's ball on defensive team's one yard line. (first and goal)

HALF THE DISTANCE PENALTY

1. If a distance penalty enforced from a specific spot between goal lines would carry the ball more than half the distance to offender's goal line, then the penalty shall be half the distance from the spot to goal line.

COMBINATION PENALTIES (Loss of down and yardage)

1. Loss of down and 5 yards.
   (a) Making a forward pass from scrimmage from beyond the line.
2. Loss of down and 15 yards.
   (a) Pass from behind the line touching ineligible offensive player behind line (deliberate) or beyond line.
   (b) Intentionally throwing pass (from behind line) out of bounds or to the ground or against any player behind line.

Official NFL Digest of Rules reprinted by permission of the National Football League, Pete Rozelle, Commissioner